LIG[illegible]H

POEMS

Jane Lightbourne

NEVADA STREET PRESS

'A luminous collection that pulses with emotional intensity and lyrical grace ... A deeply affecting, exquisitely crafted work.'
The International Review of Books.

Following the successful publication of *Bright Dust*, author Jane Lightbourne's second poetry collection, *Light Beneath The Lids*, is now published by award-winning Nevada Street Press.

Some of the poems celebrate love in its varied forms, exploring the joy and darkness romantic love brings, others are inspired by the force and beauty of the natural world. The frailty of the human condition is always at the forefront of the poet's consciousness, but with a focus always on light and hope amid the darkness.

Praise for Bright Dust

'Wonderful ... Truly beautiful and moving.'
Goodreads reviewer, Librarian

'Exhilarating.'
Goodreads reviewer, Educator

'Beautiful and haunting'
NetGalley reviewer, Educator

Contents

First published in 2025 in Great Britain by Nevada Street Press.

Print ISBN: 978-1-0682281-0-0

ePub ISBN: 978-1-0682281-1-7

Publisher: Nevada Street Press, London. Email:books@janelightbourne.co.uk Web:www.janelightbourne. co.uk

EU Authorised Representative: Easy Access System Europe – Mustamäe tee 50, 10621 Tallinn, Estonia, easproject.com gpsr. requests@easproject.com

The day is silent, windless,
white mist rolling in ~
we are blind beyond our fingertips,
but birds still sing.

I follow you,
traveller over misted fields,
fire unravelling frost,
falling to darkness
and beyond.

I am so still I can hear
the beat of wings,
snow fall from the sky,
my pulse pushing the blood
around my body;
your pulse, your blood, your body.
I am so still I can hear
the gaps between your breathing,
the pause before your words.
I am so still I can hear your stillness,
the roar of silence,
the sound of nothing.

The river,
snaking silver
through the darkness,
and who will dare
to brave its ink?
Running faster
than it runs out.

What should poetry be,
but reality,
distilled into a
single teardrop,
its dark heart
beating harder,
while others burst
about her?

Stones skipping ~
how many times?
Once? Twice?
So many lives,
dancing along
a river of ice.

If I take a step forward,
and you take a step back,
I will put my arms out
and bridge the gap.

With you, I was only passing time,
wasting it perhaps,
for I still had it to squander,
as silver coins on a pretty dress.
I knew how this would end ~
with a skipped breath, a whimper,
but I was in no hurry to get there.
Slow the minutes, the hours,
my head turned to you,
my heart hidden
in a silken box,
its pulse dropped
to a whisper.

To what end, you and I?
Such a small point;
so much idle thought wasted over it.
Only I saw us in the mist that saturated
the pale hills;
I read us in each tiny alteration
of cloud and sky,
at dawn, at dusk,
at any time, on any day.

The breath of the ocean
I feel in your breath,
and in our hearts' beat.
If we stay side by side forever,
will we still fit?

Time moves mountains, they say;
it brings down forests too.

And all the world
might stay or go,
might spin, or no.

As friends we stand,
while a thousand leaves
twist and fall,
as my hand
slips into yours,
and I wonder ~
is it greedy
to want
more?

Desire,
a blaze of blue,
bright as a blade
of fresh grass.
My head a question mark,
your body a freight train
passing over
my still, beating heart,
a train that streaks through the night,
fast as a fox,
and never, ever
stops.

Scared to love you,
scared to be alone,
I sit on a precipice,
caught between
past and future,
fear burning my wings.

One touch,
and I blossom
like a flower,
scented with
desire.

The flame ~
how it dances,
the fire;
how it twists,
and who can resist
the lure of
its dark heart,
the Siren's kiss?

Sour-sweet these cherries,
stolen fruit,
ours to bend and shape,
too good to leave, and yet we
couldn't keep,
couldn't let go, or hold ~
we lingered, savouring
the taste.

Pools of moonlight
spill across my fingers ~
we bathe
in liquid silver,
who know not
the lure of
ordinary
water.

Your face
glows through the gloom
as a single flower.
If I hold on too tight
the stem may break;
too careless, the petals will fall,
but I see in your centre
all the calm
in our storm.

I came to you
in a haze of heat,
in the shine and shiver of stars,
in all that I made you feel,
in all that we held
that was ours.

The wind may whip
these walls,
but its fury
can never
touch us,
where we lie,
invincible
in heart and mind.

With you
I shut out
the world's noise,
the clamour
that evaporates
as dew
when the sun hits,
and then there is
just you and I,
and our breath between,
and the steady heartbeats,
yours to mine.

We were
where dreams dived
with a dip
and a whisper,
a whisper of wings
through the cloud,
and their beat,
the beat that
rose and then fell
with each breath,
rose and then fell
to the ground.

If we could pause
the fall of water
mid-roar,
or the sun in its
cradle of cloud
before the dark,
then all the world
would be our playground,
and I would unlock the gate,
arms about your waist,
the slow study of sky
around us,
magic unending in our breath,
and all of time
ours to take.

Slow the steal of moon
across our room,
soft the star shine,
and we would weave both,
make a coat of finest cloth,
wrap ourselves in it ~
if we dripped
with jewels
we would not be as rich.

There comes with you
the scent of forest floors,
of pine on the hillside,
and I hear all that is left unsaid,
knowing an ocean wide
I try to hold
but runs through my fingers
so fast, so cold.

Marcus

Burned you were,
and not by the sun,
but by your own blood.
You wore no shoes ~
the prick of glass on feet
made you feel safe, you said.

You wanted the booze, the cigarettes;
you wanted me too, and
I wondered why,
until we talked,
and then I knew.

What was so strange:
I could see a life with you,
a life I could step right into,
where I would
live in another place, live another pace.
I saw this in the spaces
between your speech.

For I would save you
from the darkness,
my kiss would keep you sweet,
my lips suck you dry, like a pump.

Oh you knew
what kept me up at night,
but you did not care ~
you knew no fear yourself, you said.

And I was glad, for I thought
perhaps you might stay a while,
if only to slay these demons,
shoot them dead.

•

These sheets
I wash and wash,
but how to
blot out the blood?
There might be magic in your fingers,
and in mine,
yet we cannot.
Watched by a silent moon,
silver with frost ~
she will be
our judge.

Here we were,
at the top:
the world lying
at our feet,
the dying light
staining the snow red.
But I didn't see the glow
or feel the cold;
I saw only you,
and not the fall,
the ice around ~
could I even get down?

The sun dipped,
the sky burned,
then hollowed out;
I slipped
over the edge.

The Roller Coaster

The loops and coils of the machine,
steel against a steely sky;
higher than the stars
the ride,
and yet I felt no fear
with the heights,
only giddy, breathless,
disoriented ~
why?

And when the car came hurtling down
towards the ground,
I might have held my breath for an instant
after the high,
I might have stepped off the ride.

Before the car went too far down,
below the ground,
and it was dark and cold
and slow:
a small death ~
fingers close
around the throat.

How cold your soul
that rests on high mountains,
scented with pine,
with a breath of something sharp ~
salt, perhaps.
But I want warmth,
fire to rival
the sun's core,
that would destroy
whole forests,
if I let it.

How you move,
as heat along a turning road,
and I would run around
each burning bend,
but holding air
in the end.

Gently you pulled the thread,
and I felt myself unravel, slowly,
’til there was nothing left.

In the twilight,
my awakening;
the darkness close, but even so,
I saw you for the first time,
your soul stripped bare,
and I knew
that you
were born
cruel.

Your car, swallowed by the dark ~
a scream of tyres along
a road that snaked
through vanishing fields.
I held out my arms
and yet I could not slow that speed,
could not stop the disappearing ~
that moment when time moved,
and through it all the world went on,
but for me, time stilled,
and you were
gone.

Darker than her own shadow
it moved behind her,
standing in the shade of tall trees,
cradled in the dip in the breeze,
the warm before the storm
~
her life,
as it could have been,
if she'd made
a different choice.

The Bridge

I stand at the bridge,
half-finished,
hanging in the air,
while beyond the sea beckons,
waves laced with foam,
and I would walk …
to what end?
The question hangs over me,
the not-knowing;
there are stones in my pockets,
while my mind flies, evergreen.
I think
I am
half-slept,
half-loved,
half-empty ~
I step.

I hug the sea,
arms submerged in salt,
swim out past the rocks,
throwing shade into the deep.
Dreams follow me,
seaweed dresses my hair.
I open my mouth,
the fish swim in,
their own mouths agape,
as if they might
taste me.

Do I taste good? So I had always hoped,
but now I am not so sure.

Vast the space that fans out:
a black field
beneath a blinking sky,
dark as wine
or a bruise,
and I might disappear, I suppose.

I float up,
tied to the balloon,
not a breath of wind
to send me
to the sky.
And the flaming leaves
turn their bellies towards me,
and the dying sun
burns bright
in sympathy.

They say a heart stopped is a dying,
but perhaps it is a rest of sorts,
the escape I crave.

This heart still bleeds, but slowly,
each lie of yours a tiny cut,
until it lies empty, even of tears, discarded,
a broken net.

Perhaps this state is not meant to last;
it is merely a process towards a higher gain.
But I loved, I say, and I lost the game.
But perhaps, like the trees, you say,
you rest, and then
again, again.

This shadow,
resting in the sweetness of
notes
that remain unsung,
or lingering beneath the
scent of petals
scorched by the midday sun ~
in this
the ache of
all I've left
undone.

The Well

The walls of the well
I can't climb;
only my fingers move
over bricks
smooth as glass.

The sky is a small circle
above my head,
its blue impossible,
almost a reproach.

It's your fault, it seems to say,
You would go that moonlit route,
while I just watched
and laughed.
Who will rescue you now?

From somewhere unseen
falls a tortuous drip,
like a hidden pulse
through the twilit space.
Below me, only water,
dark and deep.

Is it rising,
or am I just imagining it?

I shut my eyes to
darkness, or so I think,
but for that bright circle,
that dances, like a golden coin,
always dances,
light beneath the lids.

The moon is blue tonight,
the air is filled with dreams.
In the darkest part of night
I see you,
in the quiet
beyond my window,
in the shadows that speak,
telling me
what could have been.

She was
an empty cradle,
waiting to rock me
to sleep
with Siren song,
forwards and
back,
to light, to black,
but sleep
would never
come.

Twilight,
and in the gloaming
things seem other
than they are.
In the darkness
shadows press,
and yet I
see
fire.

The Witches

Twilight, not a sound,
save for the soft hiss of the cooking pot.
In the houses, light, bright as butter,
and the curtains drawn tight shut.

But outside ~ listen!
A call, and then another.
I watch as shadows gather,
press forward, mass together,
push through the trees, to see

a fire, belching bitter smoke;
around it, figures,
wild-eyed, mouths open wide,
as if sending prayers up
to the sky.

.

There are
shadows darker than ourselves,
those with the softest voices,
that are buried
where we would not go,
slipping through old melodies,
hiding their charms
between the notes.

I could be a broken-backed bird
and still want to wing my way
home ~
as this heart, in pieces,
each part willing
its way back to you.

The Garden

There is a
garden,
long forgotten,
where dew
clings to
wild flowers that
release their
sweet scent
skywards,
where I wait
for you.

But in my dreams
we meet, and we
walk along
lanes lined with hedge and
laced with bloom
that scents the air
while I sleep, and my heart
knows no regret,
only that
spring will soon
come.

I wait
on foamy shores
where first we met,
empty but for
muses that sit and
comb their hair,
whisper promises
that swell
o’er rolling seas.
How sweet those songs
that make me
believe.

Thoughts of you bloom
across bare skies;
I miss the mess of limbs,
the tangle of minds,
that was
you and I.

I knew your body, your mind,
but not your heart ~
never held it in my hands,
or felt it breathe
between my fingers.
I missed that, and now
there's a hollow space
where my own heart once was,
where it's gone
to meet yours,
like a bird flying south.

Winter outside:
still the fields, dressed in white,
frosted trees, laced with ice,
water forced to fantastic shapes,
its roar stopped,
as if hand had held to its throat
a gagging cloth.

But always in my mind
there is sunshine,
where you lie untouched,
where summer comes
and never leaves,
and our hearts,
forever tied,
forever young,
forever free
to run.

If I could press
your petals
as a flower's,
preserve you as
a perfect piece
for eternity …
but we ride and we ride ~
forwards, always forwards;
only our minds
moving back
against the tide.

Fierce Hunter

Fierce hunter, you,
fleet of foot, tiger-striped,
whom I snatched
from the silver forests
of your youth,
from azure seas
sent you spinning
over the emptiness
to a world you didn't recognise,
to a world that worshipped you
as a god,
and you, you lapped it up; the cream,
grew fat with it.

I remember October,
floors carpeted with flowers,
when the wind and the rain rattled
the shutters
of silent restaurants,

when animals cowered,
seeking shelter, or even less,
a small crumb
of kindness.

Do I feel regret
now that you are no longer
in my arms,
paws reaching out;
my brave act turning its soft belly to the sun,
shrivelling in its heat,
becoming foolish?

Do I ?

RIP Theo aka 'Pickle', a silver tabby cat
rescued from the island of Agistri, Greece.
April 2020 – 21st October 2023

Earth covers your face;
I rest my head among the
memories,
fresh as flowers, watered with
an ocean's layer
of tears.

Passing through
on borrowed time,
now we go to rest,
and what was then
is still remembered,
and what is now
is best forgot
’neath rich and fertile earth,
turning over,
always turning,
’til no thing is left.

What were you to me but
a string of glorious
notes that, glued together,
couldn’t make a single tune,
and I, once so closed,
now singing, always singing,
emptying out my heart,
every ounce,
to the dark, to the dark.

Let us leave
darkness behind, my friend,
for the day is fresh and young;
and we can run along
dew-soaked fields,
through tangled hedge
and crawling bower,
so to watch fish
with silver scales
turn through wavering streams,
and their light
so bright
it blinds.

Then the rain came
upon the land,
like a blessing,
and fell onto my open arms,
like love blossoming,
and I knew that
I could never leave.

A single gull
curves over
empty seas ~
here, where
silence
has wings;
we listen to it
speak.

I know the
end of our story,
for I know
all that we are
or will ever be:
fine atoms
spinning
in a sea of mist,
hearts colliding
in darkness,
or breaking
to bits.

Our sun sinks
through its bloody sky,
and still we stand in
shadow,
wondering how to
make amends,
and if it even matters.

Watching darkness
pour over the edge
of the world,
we follow,
swimming in the ink,
tipping our heads back
to swallow stars.

The sky pulses with stars,
stretches and breathes over us,
as a living thing ~
you and I,
and the whole world
between.

My heart knows the pattern of the wind,
the endless unfold of its notes
carried on the breeze
that turns this way and that ~
all paths covered, all revealed
in the end.

The Tree

High on a hill
the tree sits,
light slanting through every branch.
You'd think its roots would tire,
through fire, or ice,
but this tree stands longer
than I've known this place,
where I've held your hand,
where I've lived a thousand lives ~
how much I've loved,
how much I've left behind.

AUTHOR'S NOTE

Following on from the publication of *Bright Dust*, I am delighted to have brought more poems together to create this new collection, with the help of the fine editing skills of Siward Atkins KC. There is a subtle order to these poems, the idea being to tell something of a story, but there is of course no obligation to follow the suggested order.

As always, the challenge with writing poetry is to deliver an emotional punch with a few words, chosen carefully, never wasted, for that would be a crime.

Those who are familiar with my first book of poetry, *Bright Dust*, might have noticed that the poems in this collection are slightly longer. There is no design behind this, and the length of a poem is immaterial when assessing its value.

Many thanks to those friends who remain staunch supporters of my poetry, and to the staff of West Greenwich Library, who have hosted such fine poetry readings and are so supportive of local authors. I am grateful to Graham Rees for his fine design.

I intend to publish a third collection of poetry soon.

Jane Lightbourne
Nevada Street Press
May 2025

ABOUT THE AUTHOR

Jane Lightbourne has had poetry published in literary magazines and was the recipient of a poetry prize awarded by Greenwich University. *Light Beneath The Lids* is her second collection. *Bright Dust*, her first book of poetry, was well received by critics and readers. Jane's novels include *Loss* and *Hannah* for adults and *A Tale of Three Tabbies* and *My Cat Called Red* for children, all published by Nevada Street Press. As well as writing fiction, Jane studied Classics and worked as a lawyer after that. She lives in London with her three children.

Nevada Street Press was a finalist in the Best of Royal Greenwich Business Awards 2023 and has been awarded Best Emerging Independent Publisher 2024 by the UK Enterprise Awards 2024 and Emerging Independent Publisher of the Year 2025 – UK (Business Excellence Awards).

.

Jane can be contacted through her website.
www.janelightbourne.co.uk
or by email at
books@janelightbourne.co.uk
Twitter handle:
@JaneLightbourne
TikTok handle:
@janelightbournebooks
Facebook
@NevadaStreetPress